The School on Bolt Street

I Talk You Talk Press

CONTENTS

1. RITA IS GOING TO LANGUAGE SCHOOL IN ENGLAND!

Rita Martinez is twenty-one. She lives in Valencia, Spain. She works in a clothes shop. She likes languages. She can speak Spanish, French and English, but she wants to improve her English. She works overtime at the clothes shop and saves her money. In September, she thinks she has enough money to go to England to study English. She searches on the Internet. She finds a small language school in London. She looks at the school's website. There are only five students in the class. The course lasts for four weeks. The fee for a month is 1000 pounds. There is a space for a student in October. Rita thinks this school is right for her.

She will stay in a hostel. The school will reserve a room for her. She pays the school 1350 pounds by bank transfer. The lessons cost 1000 pounds, and the hostel room costs 350 pounds. She finds a cheap flight from Alicante Airport to Heathrow Airport.

Her friend, Helena, is worried. She does not trust the Internet. Rita's father is very unhappy. He doesn't want Rita to go to the UK. But Rita's mother is happy. She always wanted to visit other countries, but it was not possible. She is pleased that her daughter will have the chance to travel.

2. RITA LEAVES SPAIN

Rita, Helena and Rita's mother are at Alicante Airport. Very soon, Rita will get on the aeroplane. Rita's father is still angry, so he is not at the airport.

"Take care, Rita," says her mother.

"I will be fine!" says Rita.

"If you have any problems, call me!" says Helena.

"I will be fine! Stop worrying! I am not a child! I am an adult!" says Rita. "A teacher from the school will meet me at the airport. He will take me to the hostel. I will check in. Tomorrow I will start my English classes. Everything will be fine."

"Will you call us?" asks Rita's mother. She is very worried, but she is also happy. She wants her daughter to be strong and independent.

"I think it is too expensive to call. I will send text messages to Helena. She can call you and tell you my news. I will also use a computer at the school and post photographs on Facebook," says Rita.

"How much money do you have?" asks Helena.

"I have three hundred pounds."

"Only three hundred pounds? For a month? London is a very expensive city, Rita. Is it enough?" asks Helena.

"Well, I already paid the course fees and the hostel fees by bank transfer, so I don't need much money. I will study very hard every day and night, so I won't go sightseeing very much," says Rita. "Stop worrying!"

Rita hugs her mother and Helena. They say goodbye and Rita goes to the departure gate. She turns and waves. "See you in four weeks!" She smiles. Her adventure has begun!

3. WHERE IS MR DAVIS?

Rita gets off the aeroplane. She is in London! This is Rita's first time to leave Spain. She feels very excited. She shows her passport at the immigration desk. The immigration officer does not ask her any questions. She goes to the baggage area and waits for her suitcase. She hears English and other languages all around her. Everyone is talking too fast. She cannot understand.

I must study hard, she thinks. She sees her suitcase, and takes it off the baggage carousel.

She takes a piece of paper out of her bag and reads it. It is an email from the language school.

--- *"Mr. Paul Davis from Learn Right, Now will wait for you in the arrivals area of Heathrow Airport at 4:15pm. He will hold a white board with your name on it. He will take you to your hostel."*---

Rita walks out into the arrivals area. There are many people waiting. Many people have boards with names on them. She looks at the boards and the names, but she cannot see 'Rita Martinez'.

She puts her suitcase down on the floor and waits. Slowly the people start to leave. She looks at her watch. It is 4:30pm.

Where is Mr Davis? she thinks. *He is fifteen minutes late. Maybe there is a lot of traffic on the roads.*

Rita buys a bottle of orange juice, and sits down and waits. It is now 5:00pm and she is starting to worry.

She looks at the email from the school again. It says:

--- *"If you have any problems at Heathrow Airport, please call this number."*---

Should I call the school? What should I do? she thinks.

She waits another fifteen minutes. Then she decides to call the school on her smartphone. The phone number on the email is for a mobile phone. Rita thinks that it is Mr Davis' mobile phone number. She calls the number. She hears a machine message in English.

--- *"The number you have called is not recognised. Please check the number and try again."*---

What does that mean?

She tries again. She hears the same message.

--- *"The number you have called is not recognised. Please check the number and try again."*---

"Recognise…recognise…what's that? Ah yes! In Spanish, it is reconocer…so not recognised means…oh no!" says Rita. "The number is wrong! There is a mistake!"

She opens the school website on her smartphone. She looks for a phone number. There is no phone number. There is only an email address, and the address of the school.

She decides to take a taxi to the school.

Maybe there is a mistake in the email. Maybe the phone number is wrong, she thinks.

4. CLOSED

Rita goes outside. It is raining, and the sky is grey. She gets into a taxi and gives the taxi driver the address to the school.

"Do you really want to go there? Alone?" he asks.

"Yes. Why?" asks Rita.

"That area of London is not safe for young women alone," he says.

"It's okay. My school is in that area," says Rita.

"Really? Your school is in that area?" asks the taxi driver. He is very surprised.

There is a lot of traffic on the roads. It takes more than an hour to get into the centre of London. The taxi stops in a narrow street. Rita looks out of the window of the taxi. The buildings are old and grey.

"This is it," says the taxi driver.

"Thank you," says Rita. "How much is it?"

"Fifty-five pounds," says the taxi driver.

"Pardon?" says Rita.

"Fifty-five pounds," says the taxi driver.

"That is very expensive!" says Rita. She is shocked. She pays the driver. She gets out of the taxi, and the taxi drives away. She looks around. It is raining, and there are no people around.

She looks at the letter. "Number fifty-two, Bolt Street."

She looks at the numbers on the houses. 48…50…52…

"Here it is!" She looks up at 52. It is a narrow stone building with a red door and a big window. There is a sign "Learn Right, Now" above the door. Rita looks through the window. It is very dark inside but she can see a big table with six chairs, a whiteboard and a bookcase. There are posters on the walls, but she can't see them clearly. There is a sign on the door. It says:

--- *"This school is closed."*---

Closed? Why? thinks Rita. *I emailed Mr Davis last week and he answered me. This is strange.*

She walks up the steps and rings the doorbell. No one comes to open the door. Then she tries to open the door. It is locked.

What am I going to do? she thinks.

She looks at her return ticket to Spain. She cannot change the date. It is a very cheap ticket, and it cannot be changed. She thinks about her mother and father.

My father will be very angry. Helena will say, 'I told you! You can't trust the Internet, but you didn't listen to me!' she thinks.

She has enough money to buy a new ticket back to Valencia but she does not want to go back to Spain. She does not want to talk to her mother and father, or Helena. But she has very little money, and she doesn't know the address of the hostel.

What am I going to do? she thinks. She starts to walk away, but then she sees a taxi come down the street. It stops and a young man gets out. The taxi drives away. He picks up his bags and looks at number 52. He reads the sign

--- *"This school is closed."*---.

Then he takes a letter out of his pocket and looks at it. He sees Rita and walks towards her.

5. VALDIS

"Excuse me," he says. "Do you know anything about the Learn Right, Now school?"

"Are you looking for Mr Paul Davis?" asks Rita.

"Yes, I am. Are you?"

"Yes! I waited for Mr Paul Davis at Heathrow Airport, but he didn't come, so I came here," says Rita.

"Me too! I waited for him for more than one hour," says the man.

"The sign on the door says the school is closed," says Rita. "I tried ringing the doorbell. I tried to open the door. There is no one inside."

The man sits down on his suitcase and puts his head in his hands.

"No! I gave the school all my money!"

"Me too! I sent one thousand three hundred and fifty pounds," says Rita.

The man looks at her. "I'm Valdis. I'm from Latvia. Nice to meet you."

"I'm Rita. I'm from Spain. Nice to meet you, too. Do you have a return ticket to Latvia?"

"Yes, I do. But it is too expensive to change it. I have to stay for a month. How about you?"

"I have a return ticket too. But I cannot change the date. I can throw it away and buy a new ticket – a very cheap one," says Rita. "But I don't want to do that. I'm angry. I want my money back!"

"I want my money back too," says Valdis.

Valdis and Rita look at each other.

"What are we going to do?" asks Rita.

"I don't know. But it is raining and it is cold. Let's find a warm café and talk about it," says Valdis.

They find a small café in the next street. They sit at a table next to the window.

A waitress comes to their table.

"What can I get you?" she asks.

Rita looks at the menu.

"Can I have fish and chips, and a coffee please?" asks Rita.

"The same for me too, please," says Valdis.

"Yes. It will take about ten minutes," says the waitress.

The waitress goes away. Rita and Valdis look at each other. It is warm in the café, but outside it is cold and wet. Valdis feels very bad. He took all his money out of the bank to pay for the course at the language school. He hopes he can get a better job if his English is good. Now he has very little money, and it seems there is no language school. But he is sitting in a café with a very pretty girl. She has the same problem.

I'm glad I'm not alone, he thinks.

6. WHEN DID THE SCHOOL CLOSE?

"What will we do now?" Valdis asks Rita. "We can go to the police, or go to our embassies. You can go to the Spanish Embassy, and I can go to the Latvian Embassy. Or we can give up, go home, and lose our money. What do you want to do?"

"If I go to the Spanish Embassy, I am sure they will tell me to go home," says Rita. "I don't want to do that. My father will say 'I told you not to go'. He didn't want me to come here."

"We have another choice," says Valdis. "We can stay, and try to find Paul Davis. We can tell him to give us our money back. What do you think?"

"I want to find Paul Davis." Rita feels very unhappy. She worked very hard in the clothes shop for many months to save money.

"OK," says Valdis. "We will be detectives. We will find this man and get our money back! We must find out when the school closed."

"Let's ask the waitress," says Rita. "Maybe she knows something."

When the waitress brings their food, Valdis says to her, "Excuse me. Maybe you can help us. We came to study at the Learn Right, Now school, but there is a sign on the door. The sign says 'Closed'. When did it close?"

"Learn Right, Now? The language school on Bolt Street? Oh, that closed at the end of August," the waitress says.

"Pardon?" Valdis is very surprised.

"Are you sure?" Rita cannot believe it.

"A month ago," the waitress says again. "I knew the school well. The students from the school often came here for lunch. The school opened a few years ago. It was always the same programme. Each course was for four weeks. One group finished on a Friday and the next group started on a Monday. At the end of August, one group finished the course, and went back home. They had a farewell lunch here. I didn't see any students in September. Enjoy your meal."

The waitress goes away.

Rita and Valdis look at each other.

"So, if the school closed at the end of August, who took our money? I paid three weeks ago," says Rita.

"I paid two weeks ago," says Valdis.

"The school closed at the end of August. But I emailed Paul Davis in September. He sent me all the information. He told me to send the time of my flight from Alicante so he could meet me at the airport. He told me the bank account number so I could send the money," says Rita. "He took our money! We have to find him!" Rita is feeling very angry now.

"I want to find him, too," says Valdis.

The waitress comes back. "Would you like more coffee?"

"Not for me, thanks," says Rita.

"Nor me," says Valdis. "The fish and chips were great!"

"I'm pleased you enjoyed them," says the waitress, smiling.

"Do you know Paul Davis?" Rita asks her. "The man from the language school?"

"Oh, yes. Of course," says the waitress. "He comes in here quite often. But I haven't seen him for a month or more. The last time I saw him was in August when he and the students came here for lunch on their last day. So it was a Friday at the end of August. It was the birthday of one of the students. They were talking and laughing. I haven't seen him since."

7. A PLACE TO STAY

Rita looks out of the window. It is getting dark outside.

"Where are we going to stay tonight?" asks Rita.

"I don't know," says Valdis.

"Do you know the name and address of the hostel?" asks Rita.

"No," answers Valdis. "Do you?"

"No." Rita takes the email out of her bag. She reads the email to Valdis.

"*---The hostel is a very clean and safe place for young women only. Paul Davis will meet you at the airport and take you there. ---* But there is no hostel name and no address."

"We have to find somewhere to stay," says Valdis. "Maybe we can find a cheap hostel."

Rita looks at a map on her smartphone and finds a hostel near to the café. They go out into the rain and walk to the hostel. They arrive at the hostel. It is an old building. It doesn't look very clean. There are a few lights on. A man is sitting at the reception desk.

"Excuse me, we would like to stay. Are there any rooms available?" says Valdis.

"I'm sorry, there are no rooms available. The hostel is full," says the man.

"Is there another cheap hostel near here?" asks Rita.

"No. You will have to take the Underground," says the man.

"Underground?"

"The train. There are some hostels near Whitechapel. But it's getting late. Most hostels don't take new guests late at night."

Valdis and Rita walk outside.

"What are we going to do?" asks Valdis.

Rita thinks for a few seconds.

"I have an idea!" she says. "We can stay in the school! It is empty."

"That's a good idea!" says Valdis. "Let's go!"

Rita and Valdis go back to the school.

"How can we get inside?" asks Valdis. "The door is locked."

"Maybe there is a back door," says Rita.

They walk around to the back of the school. It is very dark. Rita switches her smartphone light on.

They can see some garbage bins. The door is locked but Valdis pushes very hard and it opens. They walk into the dark school. They are in a small kitchen. There is a sink, a stove, a cabinet full of cups and plates and a big coffee maker. There is also a refrigerator. Rita opens the refrigerator. Inside is a jar of jam and some chocolate.

"The refrigerator is not cold," says Rita. "There is no electricity."

They walk through the kitchen to a small hallway. In the light from their smartphones they can see some stairs. In front of them is an open door. It is the classroom. Rita can see the table and chairs and bookcases.

"Let's go up to the next floor," says Valdis.

They walk up the stairs.

There are three doors at the top of the stairs. Valdis opens the first door and they can see a living room. There is a sofa, a TV, many books and CDs, a dining table and chairs. Valdis opens the next door. It is a bathroom. When Valdis opens the last door, they can see a bedroom. There are no sheets on the bed. They walk in and Rita opens the doors to a wardrobe. She shines her phone light on the clothes in the wardrobe. There are shirts and suits.

"Does Mr Davis live here?" asks Rita.

"Yes, I think so," says Valdis. "Maybe he lives and works here."

"So, where is he? Is he going to come back? His clothes are here. His TV is here. His books are here," says Rita.

"I don't know," says Valdis. "If he comes back, he will find us. There will be trouble."

"I hope he comes back. I hope he finds us. I want my money back!" says Rita. "Let's wait for him, here!"

Rita and Valdis sit in the living room.

"You can sleep in the bedroom," Valdis says.

Rita feels nervous. "I want Mr Davis to come back. Then I can ask him for my money. But I don't want him to come back, and find me sleeping in his bed."

They take blankets from the bedroom. Rita sleeps on the sofa, and Valdis sleeps on the floor. Before she goes to sleep, Rita checks her emails on her smartphone. There is a message from Helena.

--- *"How is the UK? Good luck in class tomorrow! Email me when you have some free time!"*---

Rita feels bad. She can't tell Helena or her mother and father anything.

They will be shocked. I broke into a house. I am staying here with a man. It is very wrong.

Then she looks at Valdis. He is asleep on the floor. He is a nice man. She is happy because Valdis is with her. They will help each other. She quickly falls asleep.

8. RITA LOOKS AROUND

Rita wakes up. She looks at her phone. It is 7:00am.

"Valdis! Are you awake?" she asks.

"Yes, I am. Let's get up," says Valdis. He opens the curtains. The sunlight comes through the windows. They look around the room.

"Look, there is a laptop computer and a printer on the table!" says Rita. "He left his computer and many clothes here, so he must come back soon."

"I don't know. Maybe. It's strange," says Valdis. "I studied IT at university, so I will look at his computer. But first I want a cup of coffee."

"We will have to go out. There is no electricity."

"OK. I'll look at the computer when we come back."

Rita takes her bag and goes to the bathroom. Of course there is no hot water. She washes in cold water and changes her clothes. Then she waits for Valdis to wash and change.

Rita and Valdis eat breakfast in the same cheap café in the next street. Bolt Street is very quiet, but the next street is busy. There are many small shops and many cars on the road. It is noisy. They eat bacon, eggs and toast and drink large cups of black coffee. The café is full. The waitress from last night remembers them. She smiles and says hello. She is too busy to talk to them today.

After breakfast, they walk back to the school.

"How will you look at the computer if there is no electricity?" asks Rita.

"It's a laptop. I hope there is still some power in the battery,"

15

answers Valdis.

"While you are looking at the computer, I will look around, and see if I can find any information."

Rita starts in the classroom. She finds many exercises for students. She starts to read them. They are interesting. There are funny stories, conversation topics and games. Rita feels sad.

I planned to start my English classes today. I would like to be here with the teacher and the other students.

She goes into the kitchen. It is old, but it is clean. She looks at two boxes on the wall. They seem to be gas and electricity boxes. There are spaces at the bottom. They have cards in them. The cards look like credit cards. One of the boxes has a red button on it. Rita pushes it. She hears a sound behind her. She jumps with surprise. The noise is coming from the refrigerator!

She looks at the box. There is a small window with a row of numbers. Rita understands that it is a meter.

She runs upstairs. "Valdis, there was a box on the wall in the kitchen. There was a red button. I pushed it. Now we have electricity. See!"

She switches on the light in the living room.

"Good!" says Valdis. "The computer battery charge was almost gone. I have found some very interesting things."

Rita sits down on the sofa.

"Tell me," she says.

9. WHERE ARE OUR EMAILS?

"OK. Paul used this computer for all Learn Right, Now's business. So there are files, letters and emails for everything. Paul Davis owns the school. He does most things himself.

"I looked at the emails. They are all business emails. There are messages to students and messages to the hostels."

"How could you look at the emails?" asks Rita. "Don't you need a password?"

"Yes. Of course," answers Valdis. "But that was easy! There was a piece of paper under the computer. Paul Davis wrote down all his email account details, user names and passwords. He is not very smart about computer security!

"But it is very strange. The last email was sent at the end of August. There are no emails in the inbox or the sent box after that.

"I looked at some of the emails from June and July. Some emails were sent to people who came to the school in July and August. They are all the same. The message doesn't change. The dates and times and the names and the addresses change, but that's all."

"So what do the emails say?" asks Rita.

"They are the same as the emails we received. So they say: ---*Send the money to this bank account. Mr Paul Davis will meet you at the airport. He will be carrying a white board with your name on it.* --- Then there are other emails. He sent emails to people who wanted to come to the school in September and October. I'll read one to you. ---*Thank you for your interest in Learn Right, Now English language school. The school will be closed for a short time. Learn Right, Now is moving to a new location. Courses will start again in January next year. I will email you in December and ask if you are interested in taking a course next year. ---"*

"But, I don't understand!" Rita is puzzled. "What about the emails I sent, and the answers I got? Where are they?"

"I don't know, but I will try to find them," answers Valdis. "Paul Davis uses Internet banking. So I can look at his bank accounts."

"How can you do that?"

"If you have the user name, the account number and the password, you can easily look at a bank account.

"There is a lot I can find out. But it is going to take me an hour or more. I am slow at reading English."

"You will have very good English practice," Rita says, smiling.

Valdis smiles too. "That's true. It's not the English class I planned to have this morning, but maybe it will be useful! What are you going to do?"

"We have electricity now, so I am going to find a shop and buy some food. That café is cheap, but I don't have much money. So I will buy some things to cook."

"That would be great. I will give you some money." Valdis takes out his wallet and gives Rita some money. "It's so cold in here. Will that heater work now?"

Rita looks at the heater. It is a gas heater. There were two meters in the kitchen. *Maybe the other meter is for gas,* she thinks.

She goes back to the kitchen. She looks at the stove. It is a gas stove.

We need gas, she thinks. *The other meter is for the gas.* Rita looks at it. There is no red button but there is a green one. She pushes it. She goes to the stove and tries to turn on a burner. Nothing happens. She goes back and looks at the meter again. Then she thinks about gas. *The gas tap will be turned off!*

She looks and finds the gas tap. She tries the gas burner again. This time there is a flame. Rita goes upstairs and turns on the gas heater for Valdis.

"I'm going to the shop now," she says.

Valdis doesn't answer. He is looking at the computer screen. Rita smiles.

He is very nice, and very good-looking. I think he is smart too.

10. RITA GOES TO THE SHOP

Rita goes out of the back door and walks around onto the street. There is a grocery store on the corner. It is like a mini-supermarket. Rita takes a basket and puts milk, bread, butter, coffee, eggs, tomatoes, some chicken and cheese into it. She takes some biscuits and some apples too. She goes to the counter to pay.

When Rita pays for the food she asks the woman at the counter, "Do you know Mr Paul Davis from the language school?"

"Oh, yes!" says the woman. "I think he buys most of his food at the big supermarket on the main street, but he comes in here sometimes. I haven't seen him for a few weeks though."

Rita hurries back to the language school. She puts the food in the refrigerator and makes some coffee. She takes a cup to Valdis. He is looking at the computer screen. Then she goes back downstairs and takes a cup of coffee into the classroom.

I will give myself an English lesson, she thinks.

She chooses one of the lessons and reads it. She answers the questions. Then she finds some quizzes. She doesn't know some of the words, and she doesn't have the answers. It is cold in the classroom.

Shall I turn on the heater? No. I will go and see if there is hot water in the bathroom now. I will have a bath and wash my hair.

Rita pushes some buttons in the bathroom, and finally gets hot water. She thinks about Paul Davis.

Someone took the sheets off the bed and turned off the gas. There was no food in the refrigerator. Paul Davis left a lot of clothes and his computer. What does it mean? I think he went away, but he plans to come back. Did he change his computer? Why can't Valdis find the emails I sent to Paul Davis, and the emails Paul Davis sent to me?

Rita dries her hair and puts on clean clothes. When she goes into the living room, Valdis looks up from the computer screen. He is looking at a piece of paper.

"Come and sit at the table. I'll show you what I found out."

11. I KNOW WHERE THE EMAILS ARE GOING

Rita sits at the table with Valdis.

"First, I looked at all the emails again. I told you that there were no emails coming in, or going out after the end of August. I found the reason. The email account has a message forward option. Every email sent to the address after the end of August was forwarded to a different email account."

"I can do that," says Rita. "I can tell my computer email account to send all my messages to my smartphone. But the messages stay on my computer too."

"Yes," says Valdis. "But this is a webmail account. It is easy to tell the computer not to keep copies."

"So you can't read the emails after the end of August?" Rita is disappointed.

"Yes I can!" Valdis laughs. "I had the address, so all I needed was the password."

"It was on the piece of paper under the computer?"

"No. No, it wasn't. I had to guess it."

"How could you guess it?" Rita thinks Valdis is very clever.

"Well, the original email address was LearnRight@posteemail.com."

"Yes," says Rita. "That's the address I sent my emails to. It's the address on the website."

"Right. And the password for that address is LR15092010. The address the emails are forwarded to is LearnRightNow@posteemail.com. And the password is

LRN31082013."

"I don't understand how you guessed it." Rita is puzzled.

"Rita! The first email password was the date the school started. The second email password was the end of August this year!"

"Oh. I see. But I think you're very clever."

"Well, many people are not very smart about passwords. I could get into the other email account and read all the emails. After the end of August, there were no more emails saying 'the school is closed for a while'. Everything changed back to normal. Students emailed asking about the school and they got answers saying 'Yes, you can come in October' or 'Yes, you can come in November'.

"Did you find our emails?" asks Rita.

"Yes. I looked at the emails he sent in September. I found the emails he sent to me. I read the emails he sent to you and to the other three students, who paid for the October course."

"Why didn't we see the other three students yesterday? Or why didn't they come this morning?"

"I looked at their travel plans. There were two brothers from Portugal, and a woman from Bulgaria. They all arrived in England on Saturday morning. I guess they came here, found that the school was closed and went away.

"But one thing has changed. Each time new students come, Paul Davis sends the same emails. He just changes the names, dates and addresses. The emails he sent to the students who came here in August were the same as usual. But after that, the emails changed. The older emails had the names, addresses and telephone numbers of the hostels. A hostel for female students, and a hostel for male students. All the emails sent after the end of August, from the new email address, have no contact information for the hostels."

"What does it mean?" asks Rita.

"I don't know. But it must mean something. I guess if students don't know where the hostels are, they can't go to the hostel managers and tell them that the school is closed. I found out something about the money too."

"Please tell me!" Rita is excited.

"Some people want to come to the school in November, December, and January. The emails to them say ---*Please send the money*---," says Valdis. "The emails tell the November people to send the money before October twentieth, the December people to send the money before November twentieth and the January people to send the money by the fifteenth of December, because the banks will be closed over Christmas."

"But the school is closed!"

"Yes. But these people don't know that. So they are sending money."

"So what about our money? Did you find our money?"

"Yes, and no," says Valdis. "I could look at the bank account. Paul paid some money to a travel agent at the end of August. The next day he took one thousand five hundred pounds out of the bank account. There was about five thousand pounds left. But in early September, Paul told the bank to move all the money from that account to another account. And Paul told the bank to do the same thing every week. So any money paid into this account goes out again. I saw your money and my money. It went into Paul's account and then a short time later, the bank moved it. I saw money from Portugal and Bulgaria. The same thing happened. The money went in and then it was moved. I saw more money too. I guess it is money from students who plan to come to the school in November and December."

"So we can find our money?" asks Rita.

"I have the bank account number, but that's all. I can't access that account. I don't have the user name or password," Valdis says.

Rita feels very unhappy. "Where is Paul Davis? Why did he take our money?"

"I don't know. He paid some money to a travel agent. Maybe he is not even in England. He could be in another country. He can send emails from anywhere."

"I am so angry!" says Rita.

"I am angry too," says Valdis. "But I have done something that makes me feel good."

"What did you do?"

"I sent emails to all the people who want to come to this school in November, December and January. I wrote 'Find another school, this school has closed. Don't send any money!' I told them our story."

"Oh, Valdis! That was a good thing to do. Which email address did you use?"

"I sent the emails from both addresses," says Valdis. "I am going to stop Paul Davis from stealing money from students. I looked at the website for Learn Right, Now. There is no sign on the site saying 'This school is closed'. I'm going to take down the site! I have the password and the user name, so I can do it."

Rita feels good because other students will not lose their money. But she feels bad for the students from Portugal and Bulgaria who planned to join them in the class.

"Can we get our money back?" she asks.

"We have to find Paul Davis first," says Valdis. "There are no personal emails on this computer. He must have another computer for his private life. Maybe I can find a Facebook page or something. There must be a way to find him."

"Come to the kitchen, and help me cook," says Rita. "You need to take a rest."

Rita and Valdis make omelettes. They turn on the heater in the classroom, and eat there. Valdis takes one of the quizzes and stands up.

"I am the teacher," he says. "Miss Martinez. I am telling you about a handsome young man. He has no money, but he likes you. He wants to take you for a walk. What will you say?"

"Yes, please," answers Rita.

"That is the correct answer," says Valdis, smiling. "Let's put on our coats and go out for a walk."

"Where will we go?" asks Rita.

"Anywhere," answers Valdis.

"Can you find the addresses of the hostels? If we have the addresses, we can go there and ask them for help."

"OK. Wait here." Valdis goes up the stairs.

Rita washes the dishes and turns off the heater.

Valdis comes back. He is carrying their coats and backpacks.

"Here is your bag," he says. "We should take our passports, money and tickets with us. I broke the back door, so anyone could come in. I'm taking the computer too. It is in my backpack."

"But Valdis," says Rita. "It is not yours."

"No," says Valdis. "But maybe it has information about Paul Davis. And it shows that he stole our money and other peoples' money too. When we find him, and he gives us our money, I will give it back to him."

When they go outside, Rita looks at the sky.

"It is going to rain," she says. "Wait a minute. I saw some

umbrellas near the front door." She comes back with two big umbrellas.

Rita finds the way to the hostels on her smartphone. They walk to the hostels and ask about reservations for the Learn Right, Now school. At both hostels the person in the office tells them the same story. Students from the school came to the hostels every month. But when he made the student reservations for August, Paul Davis said 'This is the last reservation for a few months. I am closing the language school for a while.'

Rita and Valdis walk back to the language school. It has started to rain. It is also cold. "So this was not a mistake," says Valdis. "Paul Davis never made reservations for us. He took our money, but he told the hostel people the school was closed."

"We can go to the police," says Rita. "We can tell them our story."

"I don't think we can talk to the police," answers Valdis. "We broke the door of the language school. We stayed there. We used the gas and electricity. I used the computer. I took it away. We will be in big trouble with the police."

"So we still have to find Paul Davis?"

"Yes. When we return to the school I will try again. There must be some information on this computer to help us!"

Back at the language school, Valdis takes the computer upstairs. He plans to close the website, and search the computer files again. Rita starts to prepare the evening meal. She takes the chicken and the tomatoes out of the refrigerator. She finds a knife in the drawer and starts to cut up the tomatoes. Then Rita hears voices. Someone is outside the back door.

"Someone has been here," a man's voice says. "Look! The lock is broken."

Rita is very frightened. She drops the knife and runs upstairs.

12. VALDIS KNOWS OUR PLAN

"Valdis! Someone is coming!"

"Good!" says Valdis. "I hope it is Paul Davis!" He walks towards the stairs.

"No! Valdis, please! There are two men, maybe more. Let's hide!"

"Someone's cooking," says a man's voice.

"Who is here then?" says a second voice.

"The person called Valdis must here. The man who sent the emails today. I have to get him!"

"Quick! The window!" whispers Valdis. They run to the window and open it. Below is a small roof. They climb out of the window, and onto the roof. Valdis pulls the curtain across the window.

The men come into the living room. Valdis and Rita can hear the men talking but they can't see them.

"Here is the computer. Someone's been working on it. If we want our money from the boss, we must take it. And we must find Valdis and stop him talking."

"Who is Valdis? I thought we only came to take the computer away."

"No. There's a man called Valdis. He came here to the language school. He sent emails to the next groups of students. He told them 'Don't send any money.'"

"Is he a policeman?"

"No, Rocky. He's not a policeman. Don't be an idiot. I don't know who he is. But if he goes to the police, the boss will be in big trouble and we won't get paid."

"So what can we do?" asks Rocky.

"We must stop Valdis. We must shut his mouth!"

"How do we stop him?"

"How do you think?" the man laughs.

The other man, the one called Rocky, laughs too. "Oh, yeah, Bert. I understand. We kill him."

"Right, but first we have to find him. Check the classroom downstairs. I'll look in the bathroom and the bedroom. Maybe he's hiding somewhere."

Very carefully, Valdis pulls back the curtain. He can see into the room. It is empty. He quickly climbs into the room and comes back with the computer.

"Hey you!" One of the men sees Valdis.

"Rita, jump!" shouts Valdis. Rita jumps from the little roof down onto the ground. She lands next to the garbage bins.

Valdis is trying to get out of the window but the man is holding him.

"Catch!" shouts Valdis. He throws the computer. Rita catches it.

"Run, Rita! Run!"

Rita looks up. The man in the room has his arm around Valdis' neck. In the other hand he has a gun. They are fighting. Rita can't run. Valdis is in danger.

Then Valdis punches the man in the stomach. The man falls over and Valdis jumps to the ground.

The man fires his gun but the bullet hits a garbage bin.

Rocky runs out of the back door. Rita drops the computer on top of one of the garbage bins. He holds Rita's arm, but she turns around and hits him very hard on the nose. He is very surprised. He takes a knife out of his pocket. Rita picks up another garbage bin and throws it at Rocky. It hits him on the knees and he falls over.

Valdis picks up the computer.

"Valdis! Run!" screams Rita.

13. WHERE ARE WE?

They run to the front of the building and along Bolt Street. Rita looks back. The two men are chasing them. They come to a corner.

"This way," says Rita.

It is a very narrow street. At the end of the street is a busy road. There are many people. Valdis runs into a woman. Her shopping bag falls on the road.

"Hey! Be careful!" she shouts.

"Sorry!" says Valdis. He looks down the narrow street. He can see the two men are only 50 metres away.

He can't use his gun in the street, thinks Valdis. *But we are in a lot of danger.*

He takes Rita's hand.

"Rita! Come on!"

They run very fast, but one of the men is also very fast. He is getting closer. Suddenly Valdis pulls Rita across the road. There are many cars and buses coming. A bus almost hits them. The driver shouts at them. But the two men cannot follow them across the road.

"Give me that computer, or I will find you and kill you!" shouts one of the men.

Rita and Valdis run until they are very far away. Valdis looks around. There are almost no people on the streets.

I hope they couldn't follow us, he thinks. *It would be very easy to shoot us here. We must find a busy road. A place where there are many people.*

But Rita says, "Valdis, I can't run any more. There's a park there. Please, can we stop for a while?"

They go into the park and sit on a bench. The bench is still wet from the heavy rain, and the rain is dripping from the trees. There are no people in the park.

Rita looks at Valdis. "What are we going to do? Should we go to the police?"

Valdis shakes his head. "I don't know. I really don't know."

"Who are those men?" asks Rita. "Was one of them Paul Davis?"

"No," says Valdis. "Their names are Rocky and Bert. Did you hear them talk about 'the Boss'? Maybe their boss is Paul Davis. I don't think they know very much. I think someone told them to get the computer from the apartment, and to find me."

"Why did you go back to get the computer?" asks Rita.

"The files on the computer show the plan. The files show how Paul Davis took everyone's money. If we can talk to the police, the files will tell the story. So we need the computer."

"But the man shouted 'give me the computer or I will kill you'. So we are in danger. We have to go to the police," says Rita.

Valdis is still holding the computer. He puts it inside his jacket to keep it dry.

"I have my wallet in my pocket, so we have some money," he says. "But everything else - your money, our passports, our tickets, our clothes, are back at the school. If they look, they will know our names."

"Yes. But they don't know where we are," says Rita. "We will find somewhere to stay. You have the computer. We will think of something to do."

She looks at the name of the park. "I will find out where we are."

She takes out her smartphone. "Oh, no!" she says.

"What's wrong?" asks Valdis.

"The battery is dead. Do you have your phone?"

"My phone doesn't work in England," says Valdis. "I planned to buy a special card to put in it. It is in my bag back at the language school."

He stands up. He puts out his hand and helps Rita to stand up.

"Are you OK?"

"My leg hurts a little, but I'm OK."

"How is your hand?" asks Valdis.

"My hand?"

"You hit that man very hard! I am going to be nice to you. I don't want you to hit me!"

Rita laughs. "I was very angry. I only hit people when I am very angry."

Rita and Valdis start walking. It is getting dark.

"We must find a hotel," says Valdis. "We need somewhere to stay."

"I think a hotel will be too expensive."

They walk for a long time. The streets are dark. People are going home from work. It starts to rain again.

"Rita," says Valdis. "I think we have walked in a circle."

He points to the corner of a street, and then he says, "That street is Bolt Street."

Rita looks at the street. He is right. It is Bolt Street. Rita feels nervous.

"Valdis! The two men might be here. We must hide from them! Let's get far away from Bolt Street!"

14. THAT'S PAUL DAVIS OVER THERE

"Hey! Hey!"

Someone is shouting at them. It is a woman. She is running towards them. Rita and Valdis stop. The woman comes closer. It is the waitress from the cafe. They relax.

"Are you OK?" she asks.

"Yes, we're OK, thank you," answers Rita.

"I was worried, because thirty minutes ago, two men came into the café. They were looking for you. They knew your names, and your faces, and everything. I know one of the men. He is not a nice person. You don't want to meet people like him."

"Do you know a cheap hotel or hostel near here?" asks Rita. "Last night we stayed at the school, but we can't go back there."

"Where are your bags?" asks the waitress.

"Everything is back at the school. We were trying to find Paul Davis. Then those men came and we ran away."

"You were trying to find Paul Davis?" asks the waitress slowly.

"Yes. The owner of the language school."

Rita is surprised because the waitress is laughing. The waitress is looking at the other side of the street.

"Can you see that man with the big suitcase and the briefcase? That's Paul Davis!"

Valdis and Rita thank the waitress, then they cross the road and run after the man.

"Mr Davis! Mr Davis!" they shout. The man stops and turns around. He is very tall. He is about forty years old. He has a nice smile.

"Yes?" he says.

"I'm Valdis Jansons, and this is Rita Martinez. We want our money back!"

"Money? Do I have your money?"

"Yes. We paid for a language course at your school. We sent the money to you. We came yesterday. There was no one at the airport to meet us, and there was no one at the school. You stole our money!" Rita is feeling very angry.

"But I've been in Ireland since the end of August! I came back this evening."

"I don't believe you!" shouts Rita. "You sent those men to the language school to get the computer. You told them to shut Valdis' mouth. They want to kill him!"

"You are very angry," Mr Davis says to Rita "I know you don't believe me. But, look." He takes some papers out of his pocket and gives them to Rita.

"There is my air ticket from Shannon Airport, and my train ticket from Heathrow Airport to London. The times are on the tickets. I was not here."

"Maybe you sent those men an email." Rita is not sure.

"Come back to the language school with me, and we will find out what happened," says Mr Davis.

"I think that is a bad idea," says Valdis. "I think the two men are there. They are waiting for me. They are dangerous."

"What!" Mr Davis looks very surprised. "Look, we are outside a pub. Let's go inside and you can tell me all about this."

Valdis thinks, *Maybe Paul Davis doesn't know about this. Maybe we can trust him. I don't know. But there will be many people inside the pub. We will be safe.*

He takes Rita's hand and says, "OK. We don't know if we can trust you, but we will come into the pub."

The pub is warm. There are many people. They look friendly. One of them calls out to Mr Davis.

"Hi, Paul! Good to see you back! How was Ireland?"

Mr Davis tells Valdis and Rita to sit at a small table.

"What would you like to drink?" he asks.

"Orange juice, please," says Rita. She is starting to feel better.

Valdis asks for beer. He heard that English beer is very good.

Mr Davis comes back with the drinks. He has a glass of beer too. Valdis drinks some of his beer.

"This is very good, thank you," he says to Mr Davis.

"The orange juice is good too," says Rita. "Thank you, Mr Davis."

"Oh, please call me Paul," says Mr Davis.

"OK, thank you," say Rita and Valdis.

"Now tell me all about it," says Paul.

Rita and Valdis explain again. They tell Paul they came to London. They tell him there was no one to meet them at the airport. They tell him they stayed at the language school. They do not tell Paul about the computer, the emails or the bank accounts.

"I am sorry we stayed in your apartment," says Rita. "But we were very angry, and we didn't know what to do."

"I am sure you were very angry. I am sure the other students are angry too. But I didn't send you any emails. I didn't tell you to send money," says Paul. "I hope you believe me."

Valdis and Rita look at Paul. They think he is a nice man. They remember that Paul Davis sent emails to tell people the school was closed until next year. They look at each other.

"Yes," they say. "We believe you."

"Good. I don't know what has happened, but I will tell you my story. And then you must tell me the rest of your story."

15. PAUL'S STORY

"I was an English teacher in Korea for many years. I always wanted to have my own language school. I wanted to make it special. I wanted to have very small classes, so people could practice talking a lot. I wanted to try some of my own teaching ideas. When I came back to England three years ago, I decided to try. I didn't have much money, so I rented the building in Bolt Street. It is not a nice area of London but I didn't want the students to pay too much money. I make all my own classes. I like writing stories and making quizzes.

"My school is successful. I always have five students. In a month, their English improves a lot. I am happy about that. I write everything for the classes, so I have a lot of unique and original material.

"I want to write a book for English learners. So I decided to close the school for a while. I planned to stay in a very small village in Ireland for about four months. My last group of students came in August. I closed the school at the end of August. I plan to open the school again next year. I want to find a new place, not in London, maybe in the country."

Rita finishes her orange juice. Paul picks up her glass.

"Same again?" he asks.

"Pardon?" Rita doesn't understand.

He smiles. "It's an idiom. It means would you like another orange juice."

"Oh, yes please!"

When Paul comes back with the orange juice, Valdis has a

question.

"Why did you leave your computer in the school?"

"I have two computers; one for school business, and one for myself. I left the school computer in the school, because I didn't need it."

"And why did you come back early?" Rita wants to know.

"That is a very strange thing," Paul says. He looks puzzled. "I don't understand it. I took some money with me. Then, after six weeks, I needed some more money. I use Internet banking, so I could contact my bank here. There is no Internet in the village where I was staying. I took the bus to the nearest town. I sent a message from my mobile phone asking my bank to send money to a bank in Ireland. I got a message. The message said I have no money! I called my bank here and spoke to a woman. She said all my money was moved to another bank account. I borrowed some money and I came back to fix the problem. I think the bank has made a mistake."

"Oh," says Valdis. "We wanted to find you. So we searched your apartment. I found the list of all your accounts and passwords."

He takes Paul's computer from under his jacket. He puts it on the table.

"I think you will be angry. But I looked in your computer. I could look at your emails. I saw that you sent emails to people and told them the school was closing for a while. Then at the end of August, all the emails that came were sent to another email address. Someone is using that email address to tell people they can come to the school. Someone is sending emails telling the students where to send money. We sent money in September and so did some other people. Three other students arrived on Saturday to join the October class. They sent money and, of course, when they arrived, the school was closed. We think they went back to their home countries. Some students also paid for the English courses in November and December."

"How do you know that other people sent money?" asks Paul.

Valdis' face feels hot. "Uh. I'm sorry. You left the details of your bank account. I looked at your bank account online. Rita and I were so angry. We wanted our money back."

"Don't worry," says Paul. "I understand why you did it. I arrived back from Ireland tonight, and the bank is closed. I will go to see them tomorrow. But maybe you can tell me why there is no money in my bank account."

"Did you pay some money to a travel agent in the last week of August?" asks Valdis.

"Yes. I paid for my air ticket to Ireland."

"And did you take one thousand five hundred pounds out of your account at the end of August?"

"Yes, I did," says Paul. "There is no bank in the small village, so I wanted cash."

"Well, the next day, the first day of September, someone took all the money from your account and put it in another bank account. There is only five pounds left in your account."

"What?" shouts Paul. "My bank account is empty?"

"Yes," says Valdis. "I'm sorry. Someone knew everything about your Internet banking. They knew your passwords and your account numbers. They used your information to tell the bank to move the money out of your account every week. The money goes to another bank account, but I can't look at that other account. All the money from Rita and me, and the other students has disappeared."

"You seem to know a lot," says Paul to Valdis. "Do you know who owns this other bank account?"

"Uh, no. Not really. The name on the account is Learn Right, Now, the same as your school. Someone opened an account using your school name but I don't know the name of the person."

"This is impossible!" Paul is very upset.

"Two men were chasing us. Their names are Rocky and Bert," says Rita.

"I don't think they did it," says Valdis. "We were hiding and we heard them talking. They talked about their boss. I think their boss knows about me. He knows the files on the computer show everything. He told Rocky and Bert to go to the language school and take the computer. He told them to find me and make sure I didn't talk to the police."

"What did you do, Valdis?" asks Paul.

Valdis doesn't want to say. He thinks Paul will be angry with him. So Rita tells Paul.

"Valdis and I thought you were stealing students' money. Valdis wanted it to stop. He didn't want anyone else to lose money. He sent emails from your posteemail address, and from the other posteemail address. He told all the students the school was closed. He told them not to send any money. He signed the emails with his own name,

Valdis. Of course the man who did this, the boss, was using the email account too. So he saw Valdis' emails. He told Rocky and Bert to go to the language school. They tried to kill us! We ran away."

16. IT IS VERY EASY

Paul is quiet for a few moments. He looks at the table. Then he says, "I think I know what happened. It is my fault. I was very stupid."

"Will you tell us about it?" Rita asks.

"In June, I decided to close the school for a while, because I needed time to write my book. I planned a course in July and one in August. Then I planned to go to Ireland until December. When people sent emails about courses, I sent back an email saying the school would be closed for a while."

"Yes, we know. We read those emails," says Valdis.

"I wanted to go to a very small village in Ireland. It is called Reencaheragh. Most of the country has Internet connection, but not this place. So I knew I couldn't check my email there. I wanted to make an automatic reply that said ---*The school is closed for a while, but I will answer all the emails in December.* --- I wanted to change the website. I wanted a new message that said ---*Fill in this form if you want to join a class next year.* ---

"Like 'out of office' replies," says Rita. "I know about those."

"Yes," says Paul. "They are very easy. Everyone says so. But I couldn't do it. I tried and tried. It was the end of August and I had to leave for Ireland. I was worried.

"I was here in this pub. I was leaving for Ireland the next day. Then I saw Cyril. He is a website designer. He made my website for the school when I started. I told Cyril about my problem. He said, 'I'll fix it for you. Buy me a beer. When the bar is closed I will come to your apartment, and I will do it for you'. Cyril knows a lot about computers and he made my website for me, so I said, 'Yes'.

"When the bar closed, Cyril came back to the language school. I showed him the computer and the reply I wanted to send. He said, 'No problem'. I went to the classroom to clean, and to my bedroom to pack. After a while he said, 'Everything is OK. Anyone who emails the language school will get an automatic reply.' I was so pleased. I gave him fifty pounds and he went away."

"You were crazy," says Valdis. "He found the paper with all the account numbers and passwords. He set up a new email account. He copied all your email account and bank account details. He set up your email so that all the emails went to him. He sent a message to the bank about moving your money."

"I know that now," says Paul. "I was very stupid. Tomorrow I will talk to the police and the bank. I must make everything right."

"It was so easy for him," says Valdis. "You gave him all the details of the email account and the bank account."

Paul's face is red. "Yes, I know. I am not good at remembering numbers and codes and things like that. I didn't think about it."

17. I CALLED THE POLICE

Rita yawns. She is very tired.

I can't believe I left Valencia yesterday! It seems like I have been away from my home for a week! So much has happened, she thinks. *But now, all I want to do is sleep.*

Paul sees Rita yawn. "You're tired! Have you had anything to eat?"

"Not since lunchtime," says Valdis, smiling. "We made omelettes in your kitchen."

"You need to eat. And so do I," says Paul. "I will buy you a meal here."

"I'm not hungry," says Rita. "I would like to go to bed. Valdis, we need to find somewhere to stay."

"Where can we stay?" Valdis asks Paul.

"Well, we can't go back to the school," says Paul. "Bert and Rocky might be there. Though I would like to see them and punch them both on the nose."

Valdis laughs. "You don't have to punch Rocky on the nose. Rita did that already. And we should be careful. Bert is carrying a gun and Rocky has a knife."

"Wait here," says Paul. He takes his telephone from his pocket and goes to talk to the barman. The barman points to a door behind the bar. Paul disappears. After about ten minutes he comes back. He is smiling.

"I called the police. They know Bert and Rocky very well. They will wait at the language school. If they come near there, the police will catch them."

"That's good." Rita yawns again.

"Also, the owner of this pub is a friend of mine. It is not a hotel, but he has bedrooms upstairs. He says we can all stay here tonight."

Valdis takes Rita's hand and helps her stand up. They follow Paul out through the door at the back of the bar.

The pub owner's wife is waiting for them.

"You poor thing," she says to Rita. "I'm Brenda. Paul told me you have had a bad time. Come upstairs with me. I will lend you something to wear to bed. You must have some cocoa, and a hot bath."

Rita follows Brenda upstairs.

"Rita!" calls Valdis. "Are you OK?"

Rita turns on the stairs. "Yes, I'm fine. Just tired. See you in the morning."

"Will she be safe?" Valdis asks Paul. Valdis is worried. He doesn't know these people.

"She will be very safe. The man who owns this pub is very nice. So is his wife. Why don't we go back to the bar? I will buy you another beer and something to eat."

"Good idea!" says Valdis. He thinks that Paul Davis is a really good guy.

Brenda gives Rita a nightgown and a towel and shows her the bathroom. Rita takes a bath. She does not stay in the bath long. She thinks she will fall asleep if she stays there too long. When she comes out, Brenda takes her to a bedroom.

"This is my daughter's room, but she is away at university."

There is a cup of cocoa on the table next to the bed. Rita climbs into the warm bed. She drinks the cocoa and falls asleep.

Paul and Valdis eat steak pie, peas and mashed potatoes. They drink more beer. The pub owner comes and sits with them. Paul tells him more about what happened.

"I hear a lot in this pub," says the owner. "I heard that Cyril's company is not doing well. And someone said Cyril was gambling a lot. Everyone knows Bert and Rocky. They will do anything for money. You were lucky to escape from them," he says to Valdis.

The police call Paul. They found Bert and Rocky. They took them to the police station. The police are looking for Cyril too. Paul, Valdis and Rita must go to the police station in the morning.

18. TUESDAY MORNING

Rita wakes up very early.

Where am I?

She is frightened. She looks around the room. There are pictures of rock stars on the walls. The covers on her bed are pink. Then Rita remembers.

Today is Tuesday. I caught a plane from Valencia on Sunday. I am upstairs in a pub in London. This is the pub owner's daughter's room. She is away at university.

Rita is very hungry. She looks at her smartphone. It is 6:00am.

It is too early to go out of this room, she thinks. *I will wake people up.*

Rita gets out of bed. She looks at the books and magazines on the bookshelf. They are in English. The English is too difficult for her to read. She opens the wardrobe. She looks at the clothes. Rita loves fashion. She works in a dress shop in Valencia. The clothes in the closet are wonderful. Rita loves them. The door to the room opens. It is Brenda. She has a cup in her hand.

"Good morning! Here is a cup of tea for you."

"Oh, I am sorry. I am looking at your daughter's clothes. That is bad of me!"

"That's OK," says Brenda. "She won't mind. Do you like clothes?"

"I like fashion very much. I work in a dress shop. I want to work in a designer fashion boutique in one of the luxury hotels. I need better English to get a job like that. That's why I came here."

"And when you arrived, there was no one at the school! It was bad luck. I am sure everything will be OK in the end." Brenda smiles at Rita. "Have your tea. Take a shower if you want. I am sure you are hungry. Come to the kitchen when you are ready."

Rita and Brenda eat breakfast together. Rita enjoys talking to Brenda.

I think my English is better already, she thinks. *When I talk to Valdis I have to speak in English. I am using English all the time. This is a good way to learn English. I am pleased I came to England. But maybe I will have to go back to Spain very soon. I don't have enough money to stay long. Paul can't give Valdis and me our money back. Cyril stole all his money too.*

Paul and Valdis come into the kitchen.

"Good morning," says Brenda. "Did you sleep well?"

"Very well, thank you," says Paul. "It was very kind of you to let us stay here."

"It was no trouble." Brenda smiles. "How about breakfast?"

Brenda cooks eggs and bacon for Paul and Valdis. Paul is talking about going to the police and the bank. Valdis doesn't speak at all.

"I must go and clean the bar," says Brenda. "Help yourself to more coffee."

She goes out of the kitchen. Paul pours himself another cup of coffee. "I will call the bank," he says. He leaves the kitchen too.

"What's wrong, Valdis?" asks Rita. "You are very quiet."

"I am worried about going to the police station. I broke into the language school. I used the gas and electricity. I looked at Paul's private files on his computer. I will be in big trouble with the police."

"I did those things too, Valdis," says Rita. "I am sure it will be OK."

"I don't know, Rita. I am very worried."

Paul comes back into the kitchen.

"It is too early. I will have to wait a while before I call the bank again."

"Paul," says Rita. "Valdis is worried. I am a little worried too. We did a lot of bad things. We broke the back door of the school. We stayed in your apartment. We used your gas and electricity. We searched your computer. The police will not be nice to us."

Paul laughs. "We won't tell the police that. You helped me a lot. You helped the police. They caught Rocky and Bert. They found Cyril. Cyril told the police everything.

"You were right, Valdis. Cyril did all the bad things. He promised to pay Bert and Rocky five thousand pounds if they got the computer, and stopped you talking to the police. He says he never told them to kill you. He says he only wanted Rocky and Bert to frighten you.

"You can tell the police everything you know. You can tell the police everything you heard. There will be no trouble."

The police are very nice. Rita tells the police about Rocky and Bert. One of the police officers speaks Spanish. He asks Rita to repeat everything in Spanish.

"We will type everything you said in Spanish. You can check it and sign it," the police officer says.

"We couldn't find a Latvian translator this morning," says the police officer. "Valdis, can you try to tell us in English? Later we will find someone to translate it into Latvian. Then you can check it and sign it."

"OK," says Valdis. "I will try." He feels much better.

19. WE WILL HAVE TO GO HOME

They are at the police station for a long time. When they finish, they go to the café for lunch.

Paul thanks the waitress. "You helped a lot," he says.

Then he tells Rita and Valdis he will go to the bank.

"Will you wait for me at the language school?" he asks. "Here are the keys. Your bags are still there. Please make yourselves at home."

"Sorry," says Valdis. "What does 'make yourselves at home' mean?"

"It's another idiom," says Paul. "It means you can imagine the language school is your own home. You can make a coffee or a snack. You can watch TV, or take a shower."

"Oh," says Valdis, laughing. "We 'made ourselves at home' yesterday."

Rita and Valdis go to the language school. They use Paul's keys to open the front door. They sit in the classroom and wait.

"What will happen now?" Rita asks Valdis.

"I don't know," he says. "I think I will go back to Latvia tomorrow. I don't have enough money for a hotel. I hope I have enough money to buy a new ticket."

"I am sure Paul wants to help us. But he has lost all his money too. I will have to go home too," says Rita.

"Can I email you?" asks Valdis.

"Yes. That would be very nice. We can practice English together."

"We can use Skype too," says Valdis. "I like you a lot. I will miss you."

"Me too." Rita is happy. Everything has gone wrong. She has lost her money. She must go back to Spain. Her father will say 'I told you not to go'. Helena will say the same thing. Her mother will be very sorry because Rita's big adventure went wrong. But Rita is happy, because Valdis likes her. She likes him too.

He is brave and clever and strong, she thinks. *He is also handsome. It is very sad that he lives in Latvia, and I live in Spain. Maybe I can save a lot of money and go and visit him? No. It's impossible. My family will never agree.*

Valdis is making plans too. *She is the best girl I ever met. I must get a good job so I can save money and go to Spain.* Then he starts worrying. *It will take me a long time. She is so pretty and so smart. Many men will want dates with her. And I am not Spanish. Her family might not like me.*

Valdis and Rita sit quietly in the classroom and wait for Paul. They don't talk, but Valdis holds Rita's hand. Finally Paul returns. He is very cheerful.

"Good news!" he shouts. "Good news! I bought some wine. Let's go upstairs!"

They go up to the living room. Paul opens the wine. He pours a glass for everyone.

"It was identity theft. The bank has insurance. So they will give me my money."

"Identity theft?" asks Rita. "What does that mean?"

"Someone said to the bank, 'I am Paul Davis'," says Paul. "They stole my identity. Banks with internet banking services have insurance for identity theft. My bank has this insurance. Cyril said to the bank, 'I am Paul Davis. Send all the money to a different bank account.' The bank didn't check. So I will get all my money back.

"Cyril didn't spend the money. He was saving the money to go to America. He wanted to go to Las Vegas. It will take a few weeks, but all the students will get their money back too!"

"That's good news," says Valdis. "I am very happy. Maybe when I get my money back I can come back to England."

"I don't think my family will let me come to England again," says Rita. "But I will be happy to get my money. Will you send it to me?"

"Yes, yes. Of course," says Paul. "But I have a question for you. Would you like to go to Ireland?"

"Ireland?" Rita and Valdis are very surprised.

"The bank gave me some money today. I am going back to Ireland. I am inviting you to come with me. I can pay for your travel, and you can stay with me."

Valdis is happy. "I would love to go to Ireland. Yes, I would like to come."

"Good," says Paul. "You can help me with my book. You can test the questions and exercises. We will speak English all day every day."

"Great!" Valdis is excited.

Rita doesn't say anything. She looks very sad.

"Rita?" asks Valdis. "Don't you want to go to Ireland with Paul and me?"

"Yes, I do. But I can't." Rita is unhappy. "I can't go to Ireland, and stay in a house with two men. My family will be very angry."

"But Rita!" Valdis is surprised. "You stayed here with me."

"Yes, I know. But we had nowhere to stay, and I was very angry. Going to Ireland is different."

Paul is laughing. "Rita. If you want to come to Ireland with us, it's OK. I am staying with my mother. She was an art teacher. When she retired she wanted to paint pictures. So she bought a house in a very small village. She will cook for us. She will look after you very well. She can speak Spanish. I am sure your family will agree."

"Then yes!" Rita is very happy. "Yes, I want go to Ireland with you."

THANK YOU

Thank you for reading The School on Bolt Street. (Word count: 12,769) We hope you enjoyed it.

There are quizzes about this book on our free study site I Talk You Talk Press EXTRA. http://italk-youtalk.com

If you would like to read more graded readers, please visit our website http://www.italkyoutalk.com

Other Level 2 graded readers include
Adventure in Rome
Andre's Dream
A Passion for Music
Christmas Tales
Danger in Seattle
Don't Come Back
Finders Keepers…
Marcy's Bakery
Men's Konkatsu Tales
Salaryman Secrets!
Stories for Halloween
The Perfect Wedding
The House in the Forest
Train Travel
Trouble in Paris

Women's Konkatsu Tales

ABOUT THE AUTHOR

I Talk You Talk Press is a Japan-based publisher of language textbooks, graded readers and language learning/teaching resources.

Our team is made up of highly experienced language teachers and translators, who have all studied at least one additional language to an advanced level.

This experience enables us to design our materials from the perspective of both the teacher and the learner. We consult with both teachers and language learners when designing our textbooks and graded readers, and test our materials extensively in the classroom before publication.

We are a fast-growing press, and currently publish graded readers for learners of English. We publish new graded readers monthly.

www.ingramcontent.com/pod-product-compliance
Lightning Source LLC
Chambersburg PA
CBHW022342040426
42449CB00006B/686